FLOWERS, FRUITS AND SEEDS

Angela Royston

Heinemann Library
Chicago, Illinois

Designed by AMR Ltd.
Printed and bound in Hong Kong/China by South China Printing Co. Ltd.

04 03 02 01 00
10 9 8 7 6 5 4 3

Library of Congress Cataloging-in-Publication Data

Royston, Angela.
    Flowers, fruits & seeds / Angela Royston.
      p. cm. – (Plants)
    Includes bibliographical references and index.
    Summary: An introduction to how plants reproduce, discussing buds, flowers, fruits, nuts, pods, pollination, and the dispersal of seeds.
    ISBN 1-57572-822-2 (lib. bdg.)
    1. Plants—Reproduction—Juvenile literature. 2. Flowers-–Juvenile literature. 3. Fruit-Juvenile literature. 4. Seeds-–Juvenile literature. [1. Flowers. 2. Seeds. 3. Fruit. 4. Plants—Reproduction.] I. Title. II. Title: Flowers, fruits, and seeds. III. Series: Plants (Des Plaines, Ill.)
QK827.R68   1999
575.6—dc21   98-42809
                                        CIP
                                        AC

Acknowledgments
The Publishers would like to thank the following for permission to reproduce photographs:
Ardea: I. Beames p. 10, A. Paterson p. 17; Bruce Coleman: E. Crichton p. 20, G. Langsbury p. 19; Garden and Wildlife Matters: pp. l2, 16,18, 22, 23, 25, M. Land p. 5, C. Milkins pp. 8, 9, J. Phipps p. 4; Chris Honeywell: pp. 28, 29; Oxford Scientific Films: H. Abipp p. 21, G. Bernard pp. 11, 26, 27, D. Cooke p. 13, D. Dale p. 14, C. Hvidt p. 15, D. Thompson pp. 6, 7, I. West p. 24.
Cover photograph: Jean-Michel Labat, Ardea
Every effort has been made to contact copyright holders of any material reproduced in this book.
Any omissions will be rectified in subsequent printings if notice is given to the Publisher.

Any words appearing in bold, **like this**, are explained in the Glossary.

Contents

Making New Plants

Most kinds of plants produce **flowers** every year. How many different colors can you see in these flowers? Some have more than one color.

Different kinds of flowers have different shapes and numbers of petals. But all flowers make **seeds** that will grow into new plants.

Buds

A **flower** begins as a **bud** growing on the end of a **stem**. While the bud is closed, it is protected by green **sepals**.

As the bud grows bigger, the sepals slowly unfold. The bud unfolds too and opens up into a flower.

Male and Female Flowers

Some plants have two kinds of
flowers. These catkins are the male
flowers of the hazel tree. They make
many tiny grains of **pollen**.

The hazel's female flower is small and hard to find. Tiny flower eggs called **ovules** are inside the red tips.

Grass Flowers

Grass has green **flowers** that produce
both male **pollen** and female **ovules**.

The wind blows pollen from one flower onto another flower. When a grain of pollen joins with an ovule, the ovule becomes a **fertilized seed**.

Colorful Flowers

Many colorful **flowers** have both male and female parts. The male **anthers** are covered with **pollen**. The female **style** is in the middle of the anthers.

Brightly colored flowers often have a sweet smell. Their color and smell attract insects that come to feed on a sweet juice called **nectar**.

Birds and Bees

Can you see the **pollen** sticking to this
bee? Some grains of pollen will rub off
onto the **style** of the next **flower** it visits.

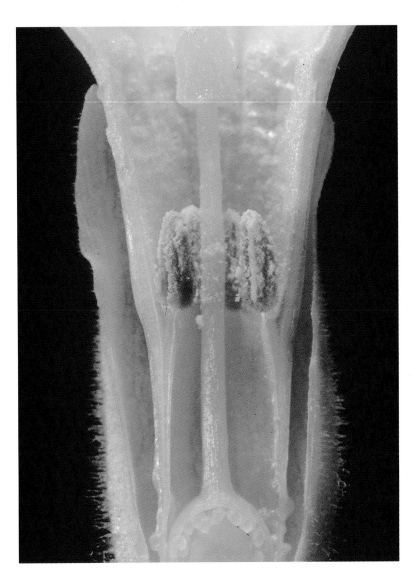

This marigold has been cut open to show the **ovules** at the bottom of the style. Pollen from another marigold passes down the style to **fertilize** the ovules.

Ripening Seeds

When the **ovules** are **fertilized**, the petals wither and die. Can you see wilted flowers on this cherry tree? The cherry **seeds** are beginning to swell.

A juicy **fruit** grows around the seeds to protect them. These cherries are now ripe and ready to eat.

Juicy Fruits

Can you see the **seeds** inside this kiwi **fruit**? Seeds grow best if they are scattered far from the parent plant. Birds help to scatter some seeds.

When a bird feeds on fruit and berries, the seeds pass through its body. If a seed falls onto good **soil,** it may start to grow.

Blown by the Wind

Many **seeds** are scattered by the wind. The seeds of some trees have wings to help them blow farther.

Dandelion seeds have little parachutes
that help them float a long way
through the air before they land.

Pods

The **seeds** of peas, beans, and many other plants grow inside pods. As the seeds swell, the pods grow longer and fatter.

When the seeds are ripe, the pod splits and the seeds are scattered onto fresh ground away from the parent plant.

Nuts

A nut is a **seed** inside a hard shell. Mice and other animals bury nuts in the ground to eat later. Some of them grow into new plants.

Coconuts grow on palm trees by the
beach. Some of the nuts float across
the water to other islands and start to
grow there.

A New Plant

Most **seeds** do not grow into plants, but this seed has fallen on good **soil.** It lies in the soil until the weather is warm enough for it to grow.

It may wait until the following spring before it begins to grow into a new plant. First the **root** grows, then a **shoot.**

Watch It Grow

Plant some **seeds** and watch them grow into **flowers**! Use sunflower seeds from the supermarket. Soak them in water for one day. Then plant each seed in a pot of damp **soil**.

When the seeds have started to grow, water the pot every few days. How tall does your sunflower grow? Look for new seeds when the flower dies.

Plant Map

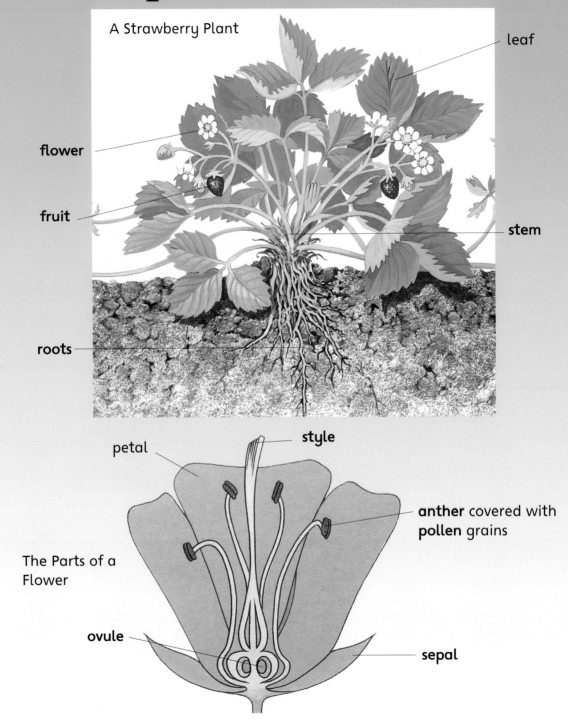

A Strawberry Plant

leaf

flower

fruit

stem

roots

petal

style

anther covered with **pollen** grains

The Parts of a Flower

ovule

sepal

Glossary

anthers	male parts of a **flower** that produce **pollen**
bud	a **flower** before it opens
fertilize	to make a **seed** that can grow into a new plant
flower	the part of a plant that makes new **seeds**
fruit	the part of a plant that holds the ripening **seeds**
nectar	a sugary juice made by some **flowers**
ovule	a female seed or egg cell. An **ovule** must be joined by a grain of **pollen** to become a fertilized **seed**.
pollen	grains containing male cells that are needed to make new **seeds**
roots	parts of a plant that take in water, usually from the **soil**
seed	a seed contains a tiny plant and a store of food before it begins to grow
sepal	part of a **flower** that covers the **bud** before it opens
shoot	the first part of the plant that grows up out of the **seed**
soil	the ground that a plant grows in
stem	the part of a plant from which the leaves and **flowers** grow
style	female part of a **flower** that leads to the **ovules**

Index

More Books to Read

Burns, Diane L. *Berries, Nuts & Seeds.* Milwaukee, WI: Gareth Stevens Inc. 1999. An older reader can help you with this book.

Durant, Penny R. *Exploring the World of Plants.* Danbury, CT: Franklin Watts Inc. 1995.

Kuchalla, Susan. *All about Seeds.* Mahwah, NJ: Troll Communications L.L.C. 1997.

Pluckrose, Henry. *Flowers.* Minneapolis, MN: Children's Press. 1994.